RAPTORS

KITES

JULIE K. LUNDGREN

ROURKE PUBLISHING

Vero Beach, Florida 32964

www.rourkepublishing.com

Project Assistance:
The author also thanks raptor specialist Frank Taylor and the team at Blue Door Publishing.

Photo credits: Cover © EcoPrint, Marilyn Barbone; Title Page © Brooke Whatnall; Contents Page © Kitch Bain; Page 4 © Kevin Cole; Page 5 © Marilyn Barbone; Page 6 © psamtik; Page 7 © Steve Byland; Page 8 © Steve Byland; Page 9 © Sasha Radosavljevich; Page 10 © George Vollmy; Page 11 © Vladimir Chernyanskiy; Page 12 © Wojciech; Page 13 © amite; Page 15 © Jose Luis Gomez de Francisco, naturepl.com; Page 17 © Helen Olive - www.redkites.net; Page 19 © Joe Nicholson, Nature photographer, Bugwood.org; Page 20 © Marilyn Barbone; Page 21 © Ivan Cholakov; Page 22 © Marilyn Barbone

Editor: Meg Greve

Cover and page design by Nicola Stratford, Blue Door Publishing

Library of Congress Cataloging-in-Publication Data

Lundgren, Julie K.
  Kites / Julie K. Lundgren.
      p. cm. -- (Raptors)
  Includes index.
  ISBN 978-1-60694-399-1 (hard cover)
  ISBN 978-1-60694-777-7 (soft cover)
  1. White-tailed kite--Juvenile literature. I. Title.
  QL696.F32L862 2010
  598.9'45--dc22
                                    2009000535

Printed in the USA
CG/CG

ROURKE PUBLISHING

www.rourkepublishing.com - rourke@rourkepublishing.com
Post Office Box 643328 Vero Beach, Florida 32964

Contents

FLYING KITES

In the animal world, kites refer to a group of raptors, or birds of **prey**. Kites and other raptors hunt and eat other animals. Kites live in warm places in many parts of the world, including southern Asia, northwest Africa, the west coast of the United States, Mexico, and parts of South America.

White-tailed kites hunt over open grasslands and farm fields.

4

Most kites, like this red kite, have pointed wings and long tails that allow them to gracefully turn and glide in the air.

Different kinds of kites live in different kinds of habitats. Swallow-tailed kites live in the southeastern United States. They prefer wooded swamps, marshes, and hardwood forests. Red kites live in western Europe, northern Africa, and the Middle East.

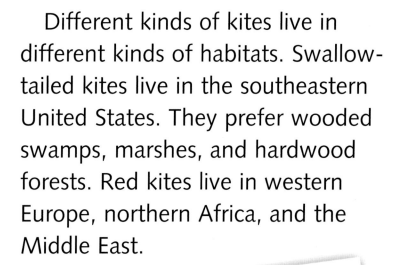

Toy kite makers named their product after kites because like the bird, they have the ability to swoop and soar.

Swallow-tailed kites move their deeply forked tails in all directions to steer and balance on the wind.

Male and female snail kites look different. Unlike this male, females have streaked brown and white feathers.

8

SPECIAL SKILLS

Like other raptors, kites catch prey with their feet. They use their sharp beaks to slice and tear their food. Long **talons** allow them to firmly grasp prey.

Snail kites, found in Central and South America and Florida, live almost entirely on a diet of freshwater snails. They use their hooked beak to pull the snail from its shell.

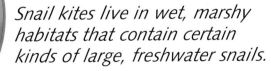

Snail kites live in wet, marshy habitats that contain certain kinds of large, freshwater snails.

Many kites catch and eat flying insects, like dragonflies. Mississippi kites come together in large groups to take advantage of plentiful food. They may catch insects scared up by cattle or a tractor mowing a hayfield. White-tailed kites have the ability to hover while searching for rodents and insects.

Hundreds of years ago, before modern garbage disposal, red kites commonly roamed the streets of London, England. They ate food scraps and stole the wash from clotheslines to line their nests.

RAPTOR REPORT
★ IMPORTANT ★
★ IMPORTANT ★

Dragonflies, wasps, grasshoppers, and other large, flying insects add to the diet of many kinds of kites. They seem unharmed by wasp and bee stings.

Red kites on the hunt soar low, searching the ground for the movements of small animals.

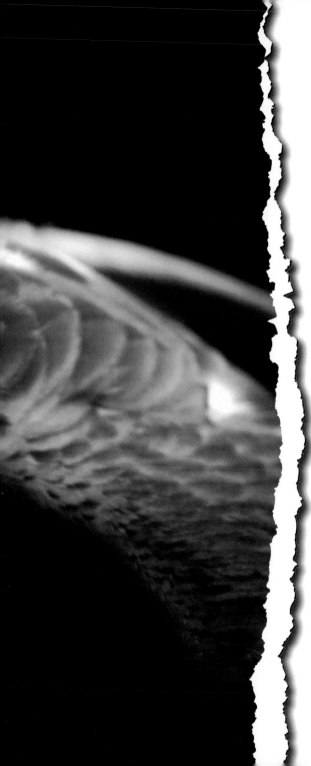

Other kites feed on **carrion**. Red kites fly low over the ground and rely on their sharp eyes to spot rabbits, rodents, and dead animals. Black kites eat carrion, insects, rodents, birds, and food scraps found in trash bins.

After spotting a mouse, a red kite captures it in its talons.

Nests and Young

Most kites build light nests made of sticks in high treetops. Mississippi kites sometimes nest near wasp or bee nests. Bird scientists think that the bees and wasps help keep pesky flies and **predators** like raccoons away. For added protection, Mississippi kites sometimes swoop down at people and animals that get too close to their nests.

Red kites need large, mature trees for nesting. Other kites, like snail kites, nest together in **colonies**.

Black kites, a raptor of Europe, Australia, Africa, and Asia, nest in trees or on cliffs.

Most kinds of kites lay one to three eggs over a period of a few days. Each hatches in about a month. For the first few days, parents provide their hungry young chicks with **regurgitated** food. They offer pieces of prey and whole food as the chicks grow bigger.

Most kites learn to fly in five to seven weeks. During that time, young birds walk around the nest, stretch and flap their wings, and grow stronger. After the first group of young birds **fledge**, snail kites may raise a second batch the same year.

The number of red kites is growing thanks to rescue projects. These youngsters, raised by bird experts, wait to be released in Scotland.

MIGRATION

As summer ends, some kinds of kites travel to warmer wintering grounds. Colder winter temperatures kill off insects. Kites that eat insects need to fly to warmer areas where they can find a steadier supply.

Swallow-tailed kites migrate to South America. Bird scientists tracked one that flew from central Florida to Brazil, a distance of 4,000 miles (6,400 kilometers).

RAPTOR REPORT

IMPORTANT

NORTH AMERICA

Florida

Brazil

SOUTH AMERICA

Swallow-tailed kites gather together in the fall and migrate in groups.

GETTING ALONG

Predators and people have a long history of not getting along. People sometimes poison or shoot raptors out of dislike or fear. Other problems that kites face include habitat destruction, **pesticides**, and getting hit by cars.

Because red kites eat carrion and garbage, people once thought of them as dirty pests. Today, bird experts teach others about the importance of nature's cleaning crew.

In important North American habitats like the Florida Everglades, improper flooding and draining of wetlands threatens swallow-tailed and snail kites.

Kites eat insects
and rodents that
cause crop damage.
Carrion eaters clean
up leftovers that might
cause disease. They also delight
with their exciting flying style. The next
time you fly a kite, remember these
marvelous birds of prey.

GLOSSARY

carrion (KAIR-ee-yuhn): the bodies of dead animals

colonies ((KOL-uh-neez): groups of animals that nest in one area, usually with greater success than nesting alone

fledge (FLEHJ): develop flight feathers

pesticides (PESS-tuh-sides): chemicals that kill insects and other pests, especially those that eat farm crops

predators (PRED-uh-turs): animals that hunt other animals

prey (PRAY): animals that are hunted and eaten by other animals

regurgitated (ree-GUR-juh-tate-id): brought swallowed, partly digested food up to the mouth

talons (TAL-uhnz): a raptor's sharp claws

Index

Websites to Visit

Soar over to your local library to learn more about kites and other raptors. Hunt down the following websites:

www.birds.cornell.edu/

www.birdsinbackyards.net/

www.hawkwatch.org/home/

www.hmana.orgwww.peregrinefund.org/explore_raptors/

About The Author

Julie K. Lundgren grew up near Lake Superior where she reveled in mucking about in the woods, picking berries, and expanding her rock collection. Her interest in nature led her to a degree in biology and eight years of volunteer work at The Raptor Center at the University of Minnesota. She currently lives in Minnesota with her husband and two sons.